STORIES IN AMERICAN HISTORY

SURVIVING

THE

OREGON
TRAIL

Titles in the
Stories in American History Series:

The Amazing Underground Railroad

Library Ed. ISBN: 978-0-7660-3951-3

Paperback ISBN: 978-1-4644-0021-6

The California Gold Rush

Library Ed. ISBN: 978-0-7660-3953-7

Paperback ISBN: 978-1-4644-0023-0

The Incredible Transcontinental Railroad

Library Ed. ISBN: 978-0-7660-3956-8

Paperback ISBN: 978-1-4644-0026-1

The Legend of the Alamo

Library Ed. ISBN: 978-0-7660-3952-0

Paperback ISBN: 978-1-4644-0022-3

The Secret of the Manhattan Project

Library Ed. ISBN: 978-0-7660-3954-4

Paperback ISBN: 978-1-4644-0024-7

Surviving the Oregon Trail

Library Ed. ISBN: 978-0-7660-3955-1

Paperback ISBN: 978-1-4644-0025-4

STORIES IN AMERICAN HISTORY

SURVIVING THE OREGON TRAIL

REBECCA STEFOFF

Enslow Publishers, Inc.
40 Industrial Road
Box 398
Berkeley Heights, NJ 07922
USA

http://www.enslow.com

Original edition published as *The Oregon Trail in American History* in 1997.

Library of Congress Cataloging-in-Publication Data

Stefoff, Rebecca, 1951–
    Surviving the Oregon Trail / Rebecca Stefoff.
       p. cm.
    Includes bibliographical references and index.
    Summary: "Read about how over half a million men, woman and children risked their lives and traveled west on the Oregon Trail in hopes for a better future"—Provided by publisher.
    ISBN 978-0-7660-3955-1 (alk. paper)
    1. Oregon National Historic Trail—History—Juvenile literature. 2. Pioneers—Oregon National Historic Trail—History—Juvenile literature. 3. Frontier and pioneer life—Oregon National Historic Trail—Juvenile literature. 4. Overland journeys to the Pacific—Juvenile literature. I. Title.
F597.S796 2012
917.804'2—dc23

                 2011020416

Paperback ISBN 978-1-4644-0025-4
ePUB ISBN 978-1-4645-0469-3
PDF ISBN 978-1-4646-0469-0

Printed in the United States of America

102011 Lake Book Manufacturing, Inc., Melrose Park, IL

10 9 8 7 6 5 4 3 2 1

Acknowledgments: Photo researcher Zachary Harris would like to thank Barbara Doyle and Joan Smith of the Washington County Historical Society; Cynthia Lenley and Joan Deroko of the Clackamas County Historical Society; Sandra Marchese of the Southern Oregon Historical Society, for her extraordinary contributions about Jesse Applegate and Stephen Meek; personnel at the Library of Congress and the National Archives; the staff of the Multnomah County Public Library in Portland, Oregon, for their endless assistance and patience; and Vasile Rady for his careful photographic reproductions.

    The author adds her grateful thanks to all of these and also to the staff of the Oregon Historical Society, the Oregon Trail Foundation, the National Park Service, and everyone else who has worked to keep the memory of the Oregon Trail alive.

To Our Readers: We have done our best to make sure all Internet Addresses in this book were active and appropriate when we went to press. However, the author and the publisher have no control over and assume no liability for the material available on those Internet sites or on other Web sites they may link to. Any comments or suggestions can be sent by e-mail to comments@enslow.com or to the address on the back cover.

Illustration Credits: © Artville/© 1995 Photodisc.com, pp. 22–23; © Corel Corporation, pp. 45, 50–51, 75, 88; © Enslow Publishers, Inc., pp. 10–11; Library of Congress, pp. 12, 25, 43, 56, 59, 64, 74, 86; National Archives, p. 101; National Park Service, p. 78; © 2010 Photos.com, a division of Getty Images. All rights reserved., pp. 27, 36, 99; © Shutterstock.com, pp. 6, 18–19, 40–41, 47, 82–83, 91, 105, 107, 114, 116; From *The Ox Team or the Old Oregon Trail*, by Ezra Meeker, 1906, p. 109.

Cover Illustration: Library of Congress

★ CONTENTS ★

Part of the Oregon Trail, as seen in Nebraska.

"OREGON FEVER"

When the first light of sunrise appeared in the sky, gunshots rang out over the silent prairie. The shots were a signal, telling people to wake up. Another day had begun. It was the summer of 1843, and one thousand people were traveling west across America in the first large wagon train to travel the Oregon Trail.

Jesse Applegate, one of the leaders of the wagon train, told how the morning signal turned the sleeping camp into a bustle of activity. People streamed out of every wagon and tent. Smoke from breakfast fires began to rise and float away in the morning air. Sixty men spread out from the circle of wagons. Their job was to gather the cattle and horses that had wandered away from the wagons during the night. It would take the men several hours to round up all the animals and get them into line with the wagons.

"From 6 to 7 o'clock is a busy time," wrote Applegate.[1] During this time the travelers had to eat breakfast, take down their tents, load their wagons, and hitch the teams of oxen to the wagons. Everyone hurried to finish these chores by seven o'clock. People who were not ready when the wagon train leader sounded the signal to march would end up at the rear of the wagon train. No one wanted to be there. In dry weather the animals and wagons ahead kicked up choking clouds of dust. In wet weather they churned the path into muddy, sloppy ruts. Either way, the people at the end of the line had to struggle through the mess made by the wagons in front.

On the stroke of seven, a horn call sounded, loud and clear, from the front of the long line. Whips cracked, oxen pulled at their yokes, and one by one the wagons jolted into motion. Slowly the wagon train stretched out until it formed a long line crawling across the landscape, two to four wagons abreast.

With luck the travelers might cover twenty miles that day—but they had many miles still to go. They were less than halfway through their 2,200-mile journey, and they could not afford to lose time. If they moved too slowly, they might run out of food in the barren deserts ahead. If they did not reach their destination before the winter snows began to fall, they risked being trapped in the high, snowbound passes of the western mountains.

Why did thousands of men, women, and children make such a difficult, dangerous journey? The answer is "Oregon Fever." In the middle of the 1800s, Americans were excited about what they called "the Oregon country." The Oregon country was a big place. When Applegate and other people of his time spoke of "Oregon," they meant the land that later became the states of Idaho and Washington and part of Wyoming as well as the state of Oregon.

Since the late 1700s, Americans had been reading and hearing about the Oregon country. Explorers who had been to Oregon talked about the mild climate and fertile soil of the Willamette Valley, close to the Pacific coast. These travelers said that rivers in Oregon were full of fish. Fruit and berries grew everywhere. Flowers bloomed all year long. Trees were so huge that six men linking hands could not reach around their trunks. Just one of these mighty trees would produce more than enough timber to build a house.

A few hardy pioneers had already gone west to Oregon. They sent back word of the routes they had followed across the vast middle of North America, which was almost completely unexplored at that time. Soon hundreds of people were leaving their homes east of the Mississippi River to seek a better life in Oregon. Newspapers all over the eastern United States described the "Oregon Fever" that was sweeping the country. A young Missouri girl named Martha Gay never forgot the day her father caught "the Western fever." Years later she wrote:

> He said he wanted us all to go with him to the new country. He told us about the great Pacific Ocean, the Columbia River, beautiful Willamette Valley and the great forests and

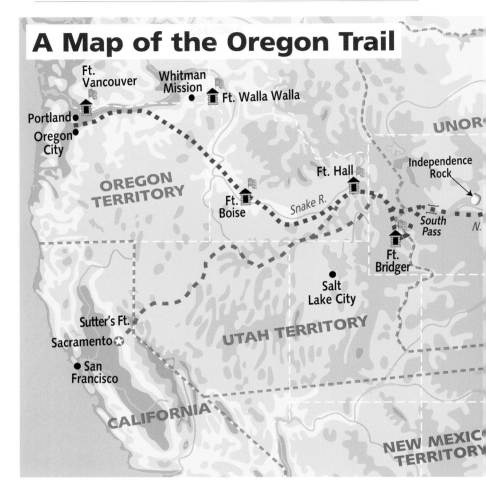

A Map of the Oregon Trail

Ft. Vancouver

Whitman Mission

Ft. Walla Walla

Portland

Oregon City

UNOR

OREGON TERRITORY

Ft. Hall

Independence Rock

Ft. Boise

Snake R.

South Pass

N.

Ft. Bridger

Salt Lake City

Sutter's Ft.

Sacramento

UTAH TERRITORY

San Francisco

CALIFORNIA

NEW MEXICO TERRITORY

the snowcapped mountains. He then explained the hardships and dangers, the sufferings and the dreary long days we would journey on and on before we reached Oregon.[2]

Gay, Applegate, and all the others who went west to Oregon were called "emigrants." Emigrants are people who emigrate, or leave their native country. The Americans who went to Oregon truly were emigrants,

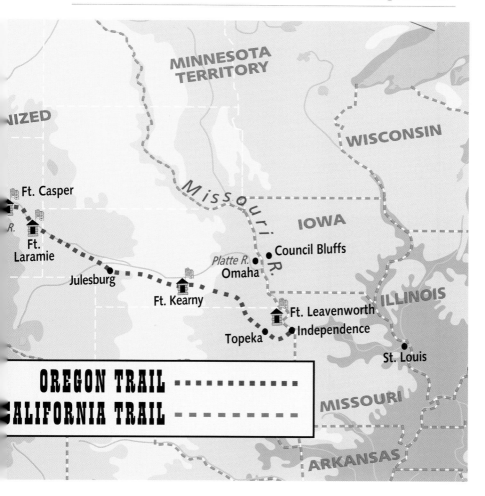

for they were leaving the United States to settle in a territory that did not yet belong to any country. Like the English, Spanish, and French colonists who had sailed across the Atlantic Ocean to build settlements in the Americas, the emigrants of the Oregon Trail set out across thousands of empty miles to build new communities on a distant shore.

Three great events shaped the history of the United States in the nineteenth century. One of these events was the Civil War, which nearly tore the young nation apart and took the lives of more than half a million men. The next event was the Industrial Revolution, which brought factories and workers to American cities and began changing the United States from a farming nation into an industrial nation. The third great event of the century was the

"Emigrants Crossing the Plains" is a famous engraving by Felix Darley and Henry Bryan Hall. It is a dramatic depiction of what life was like on the Oregon Trail.

settlement of the far West, which moved the western border of the United States to the Pacific Ocean and more than doubled the country's size. Some historians think that this westward expansion was even more important in the nation's history than the Civil War or the Industrial Revolution.

Americans of the nineteenth century wanted to spread out across the land. Many of them, or their parents or grandparents, had come to America so that they could own land. In the crowded nations of Europe, only the rich could afford to buy land. But America offered land for the taking to anyone who would go to the frontier and carve out a new settlement. Americans grew up knowing that a new frontier could always be found just beyond the western horizon. Although some people liked town life, others loved the open, free life of the frontier, where every family had plenty of living space. One Illinois farmer, for example, decided to move because people had settled "right under his nose"—although the new settlement was twelve miles away. He took his family to Missouri, but then he decided that Missouri was getting too crowded, too. In the end he joined the emigrants and went all the way to Oregon country in search of open, uncrowded land.[3]

The emigrants followed a route across the West that came to be called the Oregon Trail. The Oregon Trail ran west for two thousand miles from starting points along the Missouri River. It crossed grassy plains, rolling rivers, steep mountain ranges, and burning deserts. It took the emigrants not just to present-day Oregon but to Washington and Idaho as well, and an important branch of the trail led settlers southwest into California.

More than half a million men, women, and children went west on the Oregon and California Trail between 1800 and 1900. Half these emigrants—a quarter of a million people—made the journey in the three decades between 1840 and 1870, the golden age of the trails.

Many of the emigrants were families hoping to build new lives on the frontier, where they and their children could claim land. Some of the emigrants were adventurers who dreamed of making their fortunes in Western gold or silver. Some were hunters or loggers seeking work in the forests of the West. Others were tailors, carpenters, laundresses, grocers, or blacksmiths who planned to start new businesses in the Western territories. Still others were doctors or teachers or preachers who found people to care for among the settlers in the new territories.

Together the emigrants would tame the wild landscapes of the Pacific Northwest and California. They would make these rugged regions a part of the United States, dotted with American homes, farms, and towns. But before the settlers of the frontier could begin their new lives, they had to make a long, perilous journey across a page of American history. They had to walk the Oregon and California Trail.

LOOKING WESTWARD

The roots of the Oregon Trail stretched back for two hundred years. Ever since the first European colonists settled on the American shore in the 1600s, land-hungry Americans had been pushing westward. From their tiny settlements on the Atlantic Coast, they spread out across New England and the Middle Atlantic states, and the Carolinas. Later they cleared land, planted farms, and built towns in upstate New York and in Kentucky. Next they moved west into the vast Ohio River valley.

Each new generation of pioneers carried the frontier farther into the heart of North America. By about 1800 the edge of settlement had reached the Mississippi River—a long way from the Atlantic Coast, but still less than halfway across the continent. It would take the Oregon Trail to carry the frontier all the way to the Pacific. The story of the Oregon Trail is part of a bigger story that began with the Pilgrims and the Puritans: the westward expansion.

Long before the first wagon train set out on the Oregon Trail, people were curious about the western part of North America. The first explorers came by sea. In the sixteenth, seventeenth, and eighteenth centuries, explorers from many countries tried to find a safe, easy water route across North America from the Atlantic Ocean to the Pacific. The Spanish, French, Portuguese, Dutch, and English all looked for this route, which they called the Northwest Passage. They dreamed of ships carrying rich cargos of silks, spices, and gems from China to Europe through the Northwest Passage. But no one ever found the Northwest Passage, because it does not exist. The only way to cross North America by water is through the freezing, ice-choked waters of the Arctic Sea—not a good route for cargo ships!

Ships of many nations sailed up and down the West Coast of North America, looking for the western end of the Northwest Passage. The first to arrive were the Spanish. Spain founded a colony in Mexico in the 1530s and soon claimed California and the Southwest. In 1543, the first Spanish ship ventured north of California. The men aboard were the first Europeans to see Oregon. Dreadful rainstorms battered their ship, terrifying the crew, who expected to die on that foggy, stormy coast. Most of them survived to return to Mexico, however.

Other Spanish captains sailed along the Oregon coast in the years that followed. So did Sir Francis Drake, the English buccaneer, who searched the southern Oregon coast for the Northwest Passage in 1579. He did not find it, so he sailed on to other adventures.

By the late eighteenth century, Europeans were ready to begin seriously exploring and mapping the Pacific Northwest coast. One of them was a Spanish navigator named Bruno de Hezeta. In 1775, Hezeta was sailing along the Oregon coast when he sighted a huge river emptying into the sea. He thought that he had found the Northwest Passage at last, but rough weather kept him from approaching it. Three years later, a British sea captain and explorer named James Cook looked for Hezeta's river. Unfortunately, he sailed past it on a stormy night and never saw it. George Vancouver, another British captain, also missed the river when he explored the Northwest coast in 1792.

Cook and Vancouver thought that the "mighty river of the West" was a myth. But an American sea captain named Robert Gray proved them wrong. Gray had already made the first known American landing on the Northwest coast. On his way from Boston to China in 1787, he stopped on the Oregon coast and traded with the Native American people there for sea-otter furs, which he sold in China.

In 1792, Gray made a second voyage to the Oregon coast. He found the place where Hezeta's "mighty river" flowed into the Pacific Ocean. Gray sent his ship, the *Columbia*, crashing through huge waves into the mouth of the river. Since that time, the "mighty river of

The "mighty river of the West," the Columbia River.

the West" has been called the Columbia River. It flows south from Canada through what is now the state of Washington. For many miles before it reaches the sea, it marks the border between Washington and Oregon.

As soon as he heard of Gray's discovery, Vancouver sent a crew to explore and map the river. Vancouver's men sailed for a hundred miles or so up the Columbia, gazing at forested hills and gentle valleys on either side. The riverbanks were thick with fragrant wildflowers. Geese, otters, beavers, and deer were everywhere. In the distance rose the snow-capped cones of volcanic mountain peaks, gleaming white against the blue sky. One of Vancouver's officers called the Oregon country "the most beautiful landscape that can be imagined."[1] This was the first of many descriptions that fired the imaginations of Easterners, making them think that Oregon was a paradise.

When he sailed into the Columbia River, Robert Gray of Boston created a link between Oregon, on the northwestern coast of North America, and the United States, far away on the East coast. Thomas Jefferson— the patriot, scholar, and statesman who wrote the Declaration of Independence—was eager to make another link. He wanted Americans to reach Oregon by land, crossing the entire continent.

For years, Jefferson had dreamed of sending an overland expedition into the unexplored West. After Gray discovered the Columbia River in 1792, Jefferson grew even more impatient for Americans to explore the western part of the continent. But France controlled the territory between the Gulf of Mexico and the Rocky Mountains. Jefferson could not send an American expedition into this region, which France called Upper Louisiana.

After Jefferson became president of the United States in 1801, France offered to sell the Louisiana Territory. Jefferson bought it in 1803 for the United States. At a cost of $15 million, the Louisiana Purchase was a bargain. Jefferson more than doubled the size of the United States for about three cents an acre.

As soon as the Louisiana Purchase was completed, Jefferson sent an expedition to explore the new territory. He chose two Army officers named Meriwether Lewis and William Clark to lead the expedition. Jefferson's orders to Lewis and Clark were simple: Go all the way to the Pacific Ocean, if you can. Bring back information about the landscape, weather, and natural resources of the West. Find a good route for others to follow. Make peace with the Native American peoples you meet along the way.

Jefferson wanted Lewis and Clark to pave the way for American settlers to move west across the Mississippi. He also hoped that the two explorers and their expedition would reach the Pacific Ocean. If Lewis and Clark made it all the way to the ocean, the United States would have some claim to the Pacific Northwest. The British were already exploring the Northwest from their Canadian colony. Jefferson did not want the British to end up controlling the Northwest.

With about forty men under their command, Lewis and Clark set out in the spring of 1804. Their journey began near St. Louis, where the Missouri River flows down from the northwest and empties into the Mississippi River. Both banks of the Mississippi were dotted with settlements. Many of the people who lived along the Mississippi were already looking westward, wondering what the new lands beyond the horizon were like. Lewis and Clark would be the first to tell them.

Bells rang joyously in September 1806 when the Lewis and Clark expedition returned to St. Louis. These weary explorers had covered some six thousand miles of

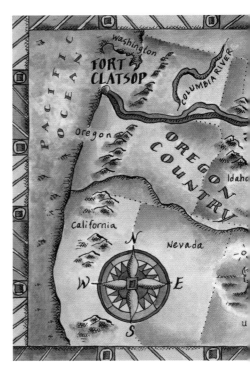

This map shows the trail of the Lewis and Clark Expedition.

unknown territory. They had gone up the Missouri River through the Dakotas. They had crossed the high plains and mountains of what is now Montana. They had scrambled through the steep Bitterroot Range of the Rocky Mountains in present-day Idaho. They had journeyed west down the Snake and Columbia rivers through the Oregon country. Finally, as Jefferson had hoped, they had reached the shore of the Pacific Ocean.

The Lewis and Clark expedition spent the winter of 1805–06 on the Pacific Coast of Oregon. They built a fort for shelter from the winter rains and named it Fort Clatsop in honor of the Clatsop, a Native American tribe of the

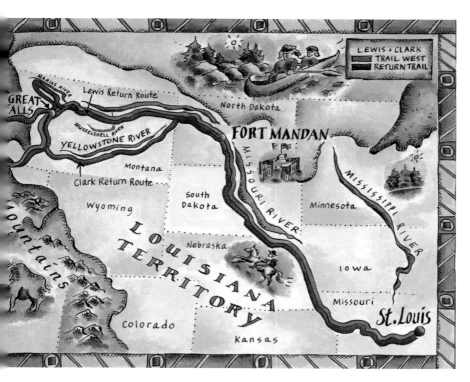

area. When spring came, the Lewis and Clark expedition turned around and began the long journey all the way back to St. Louis. They were the first Americans to cross the continent, and they blazed a trail that others would soon follow.

Lewis and Clark brought back a wealth of useful information about the West. The two captains had kept detailed journals of the trip. These journals contained hundreds of pages of notes, drawings, and maps. Americans were desperately eager to learn about the mysterious, beckoning West. When a book based on the journals of Lewis and Clark was published in 1814, it became a bestseller. The book included a map of western North America drawn by Clark. That map was one of the most important maps ever made. In the years to come, it would guide thousands of settlers across the Rocky Mountains and into the Oregon country, even though it contained some major errors.

Fur brought the next wave of explorers into the Oregon country. Gray, Captain Vancouver's crew, and members of the Lewis and Clark expedition had all reported seeing lots of otter and beaver in the Pacific Northwest. The skins of otters and beavers were valuable, because tailors in Europe and the United States used them to make waterproof hats and capes. Trappers had already killed many of the beavers in eastern North America. Soon after the return of Lewis and Clark, however, fur trappers headed west into the Rocky Mountains and beyond.

William Clark (top left) and Meriwether Lewis (bottom right) led the first United States expedition across North America, from St. Louis to the Pacific Coast of Oregon and back again.

In 1811, an eastern fur dealer named John Jacob Astor sent men to the mouth of the Columbia River to establish a fur-trading post. They built Fort Astoria, the oldest permanent American settlement in the West, not far from the mossy remains of Lewis and Clark's Fort Clatsop. Today the city of Astoria, Oregon, stands on the site of Fort Astoria.

Robert Stuart, one of Astor's men, made an important discovery on his way back from the West. He found South Pass, a thirty-mile-wide pass through the Rocky Mountains. South Pass is a gentle slope, not a steep scramble like many other mountain passes. Later, South Pass would become part of the Oregon Trail. It was the only pass then known through which wagons could travel. Emigrants were thankful for Stuart's discovery as they easily guided their heavy wagons through the highest mountains in North America.

Fort Astoria was the victim of a quarrel between the United States and Great Britain. When the War of 1812 broke out between Britain and the United States, British forces in the Northwest took control of Fort Astoria. After the war, both Great Britain and the United States claimed the Pacific Northwest. In 1818, the two countries agreed to a joint claim. This meant that neither country completely controlled Oregon, and people from both countries were free to go there.

At first, though, the British outnumbered the Americans. A handful of Americans had reached Oregon

Members of the Lewis and Clark expedition reported seeing lots of otter and beaver in the Pacific Northwest. The skins of these animals were a valuable commodity, because the skins were used to make waterproof hats and capes.

by ship, but many more British and Canadian fur trappers and traders were active there. In 1824, a British fur-trading firm called the Hudson's Bay Company built a large post named Fort Vancouver on the north bank of the Columbia River. The Hudson's Bay Company already controlled the fur trade throughout Canada. Through Fort Vancouver, the company hoped to gather furs from all over the Pacific Northwest, from California to Alaska.

Today Fort Vancouver is part of the city of Vancouver, Washington, across the Columbia from Portland, Oregon. In 1824, however, there were no cities in Oregon country. The only dwellings around Fort Vancouver were a few villages of the Native American Cayuse people.

In the wilderness, Fort Vancouver seemed like a fine place indeed. The fort was surrounded by a high log wall that enclosed more than forty buildings. It had a wine cellar and a library, complete with magazines all the way from London, England. In the center of the fort stood a handsome house with a cannon on either side and a flower garden in front. Here lived the man sent by the Hudson's Bay Company to manage the fort and the whole district. He was six feet four inches tall, with piercing gray eyes and a mane of white hair. His name was Dr. John McLoughlin.

McLoughlin's job was to gather furs for the Hudson's Bay Company. He did this in two ways: by sending out white trappers and by trading with the Native Americans. But McLoughlin had another job as well. The British wanted him to discourage Americans from settling in the Oregon country. Fortunately for the Americans, McLoughlin did not do this job very well. He was a kind and generous man, and when American explorers and emigrants began arriving in Oregon, McLoughlin gave them shelter, supplies, and advice. Many people who had lost everything on the way to Oregon were able to make a fresh start in the new territory because of McLoughlin's kindness.

During the 1820s, more American trappers and traders began making their way overland into the Oregon country. Known as "mountain men," these wandering adventurers dressed in animal skins and lived off the land. They roamed far and wide through the remotest parts of the West, often with Native American companions. In 1824, a mountain man named Jedediah Smith rediscovered the South Pass that Stuart had found a dozen years before. The mountain men knew more about the West than anyone else. Some of them, such as William Sublette, Jim Bridger, and Kit Carson, later guided emigrants along the Oregon Trail.

Throughout the 1820s, McLoughlin was busy around Fort Vancouver. In 1827, he built the Pacific Northwest's first sawmill, to turn logs into planks for building. The next year he built a mill for grinding wheat into flour. In 1829, he established a post near a waterfall on the Willamette River, south of Fort Vancouver. This small settlement was the beginning of Oregon City. That same year, McLoughlin allowed a group of French Canadian trappers to settle in the

Willamette Valley. Slowly, one small step at a time, Oregon country was becoming settled. But the rush of emigrants from the United States was still a few years in the future.

By the end of the 1820s, many Americans had read about the Lewis and Clark expedition. They had studied Clark's map. They had also heard stories about Oregon's good hunting and rich soil.

Across the United States, more and more people were interested in the Oregon country. Some simply wanted to homestead in a wide-open new territory. Others felt patriotic. They wanted Oregon to become part of the United States. Before that could happen, there had to be more Americans in Oregon. The time was right for Americans to begin settling in Oregon. The Oregon Trail was ready to be born.

3

THE GREAT MIGRATION BEGINS

The flow of Americans into Oregon started with a small trickle in 1832. That year 110 soldiers of the U.S. Army, led by Captain Benjamin Bonneville, made their way over the great Rocky Mountains and through Idaho into what is now Washington State. The arrival of the soldiers sent a message to the British and Native Americans. It meant that Americans were coming to the Pacific Northwest, and they were coming to stay.

That same year, Nathaniel J. Wyeth led the first party of American settlers overland to Oregon. Like Captain Robert Gray, Wyeth came from Boston. He had heard that the waters of the Pacific Northwest teemed with fish, and he was interested in starting a fishing business there. Wyeth hired William Sublette, a mountain man who had explored the West gathering beaver furs, to guide him and his companions to Oregon. Sublette led Wyeth's group through the western mountains along trails that had been used for centuries by buffalo and Native Americans.

When Wyeth reached Fort Vancouver, he saw that the Columbia and Willamette rivers really were full of fish—especially salmon, the main food of the local Native Americans. Some of the salmon were more than a dozen feet long. They were so big that the only way to get them out of the water was to pull them out with horses.

Wyeth decided to start a business catching and drying Oregon fish. First, though, he returned to Boston to get the equipment he needed. Then, in 1834, he headed back across the country to Oregon. On the way to Oregon, Wyeth and his men built an outpost in what is now Idaho. They called it Fort Hall. In the years ahead, Fort Hall would become an important landmark on the Oregon Trail.

After building Fort Hall, Wyeth continued on his way to Oregon. There he set up his fishing business on Sauvie Island, just across the Columbia River from Fort Vancouver. One of the men who came to Oregon with Wyeth, a preacher named Jason Lee, wanted to spread Christianity among the Native Americans. Lee started a mission in the Willamette Valley on the site of present-day Salem, the capital of Oregon.

Two years later, in 1836, another group of missionaries arrived at Fort Vancouver. They were Dr. Marcus Whitman and his wife, Narcissa, and the Reverend Henry Spalding and his wife, Eliza. They told John McLoughlin that they had come to the Oregon country to build a mission where they would teach Christianity to the Native Americans. McLoughlin advised them to settle near the Columbia River in the eastern part of the Oregon country. The Whitmans followed McLoughlin's advice and set up their mission a few miles from where the city of Walla Walla, Washington, stands today.

The women of the Whitman party were the first white women to cross the Rocky Mountains. There was also another important "first" in the Whitman party. The Whitmans and Spaldings were the first emigrants to bring their wagons all the way to Oregon. Wyeth had left his wagons at Fort Hall. He carried his goods on pack animals for the rest of the trip, because he was afraid that wagons would break apart on the steep, rough trails. The Whitman group proved that wagons could survive the journey. Nearly all the emigrants who came later would bring wagons.

Wyeth and the Whitmans had taken a different route to the Pacific Northwest from the one Meriweather Lewis and William Clark had pioneered. When Lewis and Clark went to Oregon in 1804–05, they traveled northwest across the high plains of the Dakotas and Montana. But between 1804 and the 1830s, the Native American Blackfoot nation had become very powerful in the northern plains. Hoping to keep whites from moving into their land, the Blackfoot closed the area to white travelers. For this reason, Wyeth and the Whitman group took a different route. In the years that followed, as people began to follow them west, that route became known as the Oregon Trail.

The Oregon Trail had many names. Some people called it the Oregon Trace (*trace* was another word for "trail" or "path"). Others called it the Emigrant Road. Still others called it the Platte River Road, because it ran next to the Platte River for many miles. The Native American name for the wagon route that the whites created was the Great Medicine Road. But to most people it was Oregon Trail, or the Oregon and California Trail.

Americans started going to California around the time they started going to Oregon. At the time, California was part of Mexico, which had just won its freedom from Spain. California was so large that there seemed to be plenty of room for American as well as Mexican settlers.

American emigrants bound for California had four choices. They could go by sea, around South America and up to the California coast—an expensive and dangerous journey. They could travel by sea to Central America, cross from the Atlantic to the Pacific Coast in what is now Panama or Nicaragua, and then sail north to California. They could travel overland to southern California along the Santa Fe Trail, an old Spanish route that led through the high deserts, plateaus, and canyons of the Southwest. Finally, if they wanted to go to central or northern California, they could take the Oregon Trail. The Oregon Trail forked after it crossed the Rocky Mountains. The northern fork went to Oregon, and the southern fork went to California. That is why the Oregon Trail is also known as the Oregon and California Trail. Far more of the people who set out on the trail were headed for California than for Oregon.

The Oregon Trail started in communities along the Missouri River. These communities were called "jumping-off places" for the journey west. At first, the busiest jumping-off place was Independence, Missouri. During the early years of the Oregon Trail, most of the emigrants who traveled the Oregon Trail left from Independence. After 1849, many emigrants left from jumping-off places farther north.

From Independence, the trail headed northwest across the Great Plains. The emigrants might have wanted to settle on the plains, but the U.S. Congress had set aside the Great Plains as Indian Territory. Whites could pass through Indian Territory on their way to other places farther west, but they could not settle there. Congress did not start opening up the vast Indian Territory to white settlers until the 1850s and 1860s. By that time, the far West had already been settled by the pioneers of the Oregon Trail.

As the Oregon Trail passed through Indian Territory, it led northwest across a corner of what is now the state of Kansas, and then into Nebraska. The travelers marveled at the tall-grass prairie that surrounded them on all sides. The thick, tough grasses grew as high as a tall man. The prairie grasses tangled in the wagon wheels and made it hard for people to find their way. Children who wandered away from the wagons became lost in the green forest of grass. Sometimes the only way a wagon-train leader could see over the waving grass was to stand on top of a wagon. "One day we rode on for hours without seeing a tree or bush," wrote Francis Parkman, who traveled the Oregon

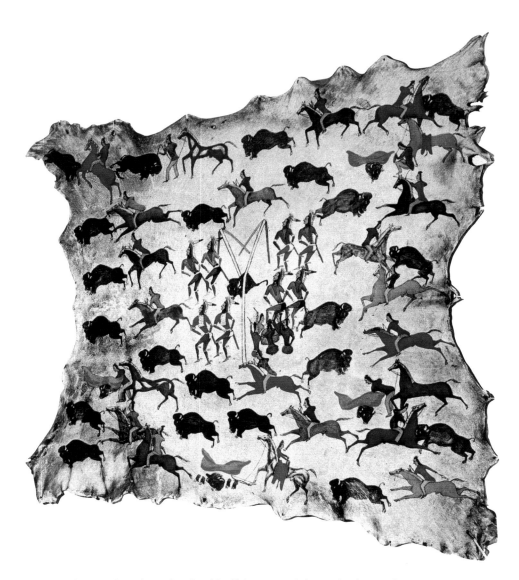

At one time, huge herds of buffalo roamed the High Plains. This is a Native American depiction of a buffalo hunt.

Trail in 1846.[1] In the spring, though, the prairie was lovely, sprinkled with wildflowers of many colors. Some travelers thought that it looked like a huge, bright quilt.

About two hundred miles from Independence, the Oregon Trail came to the Platte River—or "Big Muddy," as some emigrants called the river. The water of this river was so full of sand, Parkman said, that when he drank the water, it scratched his teeth. The trail ran along the broad, brown Platte for the next 450 miles, through Nebraska and into what is now Wyoming.

Along the way, the landscape became drier and more open—"a barren trackless waste," Parkman called it.[2] The ground was hard and dusty, and trees were very rare. The tall, waving grasses of the Great Plains gave way to the shorter grasses of the High Plains. Now the travelers could see for miles and miles in all directions.

The High Plains brought new surprises. On either side of the trail were clusters of small earthen mounds with holes in them. Small brown animals kept bobbing up out of these holes, whistling to one another and scampering from hole to hole. These busy creatures were prairie dogs, who lived in "towns" of tunnels under the prairie. No one from the eastern United States had ever seen prairie dogs before. Children on the Oregon Trail were especially fascinated by the antics of the lively prairie dogs.

Then there were the buffalo. At that time, huge herds of buffalo roamed the High Plains, often coming to the Platte River to drink. The emigrants were amazed to see the prairie black with buffalo all the way to the horizon. White buffalo skulls were scattered among the grass.

Unlike the prairie dogs, the buffalo could be dangerous. Stampeding herds of buffalo sometimes charged right through wagon trains. An emigrant who took the Oregon Trail in 1841 had a close escape from a charging buffalo herd. He wrote:

> One night when we were encamped on the South Fork of the Platte they came in such droves that we had to sit up and fire guns and make what fires we could to keep them from running over us and trampling us into the dust. We could hear them thundering all night long. The ground fairly trembled with vast approaching bands, and if they had not been diverted, wagons, animals, and emigrants would have been trodden under their feet.[3]

The buffalo were dangerous, but they were also useful to the emigrants. Jesse Applegate told how the men and boys of his wagon train would grab their rifles and rush to the hunt whenever buffalo were sighted in the distance. Fresh buffalo meat was a welcome addition to wagon-train meals. The buffalo helped in another way, too. Trees were so scarce on the prairie that the emigrants could not find wood for cooking fires. They did what the Native Americans of the region had learned to do: They burned dried buffalo dung, which they called "buffalo chips." The buffalo chips made good fuel.

Near the western edge of the plains, the trail entered a landscape that seemed strange and wild to emigrants from the gentle, rolling hills and forested valleys of the

East. Outcrops of weathered rock jutted harshly from the dry, barren prairie. Some of these rocks were so large that they could be seen from far away. Travelers on the Oregon Trail gave names to some of these rock formations. The most famous was Chimney Rock, a landmark along the trail. Chimney Rock was a large pyramid-shaped slab of reddish rock from which a 110-foot spire rose straight up. People coming along the trail could see Chimney Rock from forty or fifty miles away. The first person in each group of emigrants who glimpsed Chimney Rock in the distance whooped and hollered with excitement.

Farther along the trail was Independence Rock, another landmark. Independence Rock was a giant boulder half buried in the earth. Early explorers and fur trappers had carved their names on the rock. Emigrants on the Oregon Trail added their names, carving them or writing them with paint or axle grease. Thousands of emigrants signed their names on Independence Rock, which some people called the Great Register of the Oregon Trail.

Soon the trail was moving steadily up into the Rocky Mountains, a spine of high peaks that formed a wall between the Plains and the West. Stern snow-capped peaks stretched along the horizon. At South Pass, where the Oregon Trail crossed from the eastern to the western side of the mountains, the emigrants rejoiced, because they knew that their journey was about half completed.

This is the prairie near Chimney Rock in Nebraska. Travelers marveled at the tall-grass prairie that surrounded them on all sides.

Some of the landmarks along the Oregon Trail had been built by humans. Fur traders built trading posts that became way stations on the trail. Emigrants could rest at these outposts, or buy last-minute supplies (at very high prices), leave mail to be carried back to the States. Sometimes U.S. soldiers were sent to the forts to control the local Native Americans.

Fort Kearny, in what is now Nebraska, was the first fort that emigrants came to as they traveled along the trail. There were three posts in Wyoming: Fort Laramie and Fort Caspar were on the east side of the Rocky Mountains, and Fort Bridger on the west side of South Pass. Fort Hall, the post that Wyeth had built in Idaho, was another resting place on the trail. At Fort Hall, emigrants who had not decided whether they were going to Oregon or California had to make up their minds.

Emigrants bound for California left the Oregon Trail—sometimes near Fort Bridger but more often at or near Fort Hall. The California-bound emigrants traveled southwest across the Nevada desert to the Sierra Nevada mountain range. After struggling up through the passes of the Sierra Nevadas, they went down tree-covered slopes toward the settlements of Sacramento and San Francisco.

Oregon-bound travelers headed northwest from Fort Hall. The Oregon Trail followed the course of the Snake River through Idaho. Unlike the broad and gentle Platte, the Snake River was a fast-moving torrent that sometimes flowed through deep, narrow canyons. Emigrants had a

Fording rivers could be a stiff challenge for the emigrants. In this drawing, two covered wagons are being ferried across the Platte River in Wyoming. This drawing was created by Daniel A. Jenks in 1859.

hard time getting to the river when they needed water, but there were no other sources of water; the land was dry and unwelcoming. The trail was steep and treacherous in places. People and animals could lose their footing on slopes of loose rock. This stretch of the trail was the most difficult that the travelers had encountered.

But worse was ahead. When the Snake River canyon became too steep and rough for travelers, the trail left the river and cut across what is now the northeastern corner of Oregon. Here the trail crossed the Blue Mountains. These mountains are not as tall as the Rockies or the Sierra Nevadas—but they are extremely rugged. In places the path up a cliff or mountain ridge was so steep that emigrants had to unload their wagons and carry their goods to the top by hand. The oxen simply could not pull loaded wagons up such steep hills.

On the other side of each hill, the road went down just as steeply. For the emigrants, going down a hill was just as hard as coming up. The men clung to ropes and lowered each wagon carefully. If the men lost their grip on the ropes, the wagon could run away out of control.

The Oregon Trail came down out of the Blue Mountains not far from the Whitman mission at Walla Walla. Here the trail branched again. Emigrants who were going to the country around Puget Sound, in what is now the state of Washington, split off from the main trail to travel northwest through the Cascade Mountains.

Farther along the trail was Independence Rock. Early explorers and fur trappers had carved their names on the rock. Thousands of emigrants on the`Oregon Trail added their names, carving them or writing them with paint or axle grease.

Most of the emigrants, though, were headed for the Willamette Valley in western Oregon. They followed the Oregon Trail along the Columbia River for two hundred miles to a place called the Dalles. Here the river plunged over a waterfall into a mighty gorge, and the trail disappeared. The way to the Willamette Valley was blocked by the dense fir forests and steep slopes of Mount Hood and the other peaks of the Cascade range.

After coming so far through so many difficulties, however, the emigrants were not about to give up. They loaded their wagons, livestock, and goods onto rafts or Native American canoes and launched themselves into the dangerous rapids of the Columbia. They hoped to reach Fort Vancouver and the Willamette River by water. Many emigrants lost their possessions—and their lives— in the wild waves.

The journey west was not an easy one. For the first travelers to Oregon and California, the trail was not clearly marked, as it was for those who came later. The early emigrants were truly heading into the unknown.

A few emigrants made their way into the Oregon country in the late 1830s, following in the footsteps of Wyeth and the Whitmans. A group that arrived in Oregon in 1839 was known as the Peoria party, because the emigrants were from Peoria, Illinois. By 1840, there were about five hundred Americans in Oregon, mostly in the Willamette Valley. Many of

Banks of the Snake River, Twin Falls, Idaho. The Snake River was a fast-moving torrent that sometimes flowed through deep, narrow canyons.

them had come by ship. That year, fewer than twenty people made the overland journey to Oregon. But the great days of the Oregon Trail were about to begin.

In 1841, a wagon train of about seventy people left Missouri. Half of them were headed for California, lured by letters from an earlier emigrant who wrote back to the United States about the good life near San Francisco. The other half wanted to get to Oregon. None of them knew anything about the way west. "Our ignorance of the route was complete," recalled John Bidwell, a twenty-one-year-old teacher who was bound for California.[4] Fortunately, the emigrants hired Thomas "Broken Hand" Fitzpatrick, a mountain man and fur trapper, to guide them through the Rocky Mountains. A few people in the group gave up and turned back to Missouri while they were still on the plains, but the rest pushed on and reached their destinations.

About one hundred people traveled to Oregon along the trail in 1842. Their leader was Elijah J. White, the first official that the U.S. government sent into the Oregon country. White was an Indian agent, which meant that he was in charge of all dealings between the Native American inhabitants of Oregon and the American settlers. He advertised in Missouri for emigrants to make up a wagon train so that he would have company on the journey.

White's wagon train included a number of families with young children. "Broken Hand" Fitzpatrick, who had guided the 1841 emigrant party, guided White's group from Fort Laramie to Fort Hall for $500. Now that the beaver had almost disappeared from many parts of the West because of hunting and trapping, Fitzpatrick and the other mountain men were learning that they could make money from the emigrants.

Two of the 1842 emigrants died on the trail. One was accidentally shot, and the other drowned while crossing the Snake River. The others, however, made it safely through to Oregon. Reaching the West overland was still a risky adventure, but people were learning that it was not impossible.

That same year, Congress sent a young army officer named John Charles Frémont to explore and map the territory along the Oregon Trail. When news of Frémont's explorations spread through the United States, people became certain that the U.S. government planned to make a strong claim to Oregon. Why else would the government send a military team to make maps? "Oregon fever" spread like wildfire as people spoke with confidence of the day when the Oregon country would become part of the United States.

By the spring of 1843, more than a thousand people had gathered in the jumping-off places along the Missouri River. They had come from all over the United States with their wagons and livestock and household goods—and their hopes and dreams for a bright new future. Their eyes and thoughts were turned westward,

Most of the emigrants were headed for the Willamette Valley in western Oregon.

toward Oregon and California. As soon as the spring snows melted, the caravan of 120 wagons set off across the prairie, headed toward the sunset. The Great Migration had begun. Every spring after that, for many years, long wagon trains headed westward on the Oregon Trail.

GETTING STARTED

W ho were these people who set out to cross the continent on the Oregon Trail? Most of them were young—between sixteen and thirty-five years old. A large number of single men made the journey, and so did a few single women, but most of the emigrants were families traveling together. More than half the emigrants to Oregon were women and children.

Quite a few of the emigrants came from what was then the western part of the United States: Indiana, Illinois, Iowa, and Missouri. Some of the emigrants came from farther east: from New York and New Hampshire and the Carolinas. All of them shared the dream of free land and new opportunities in the West.

The emigrants shared something else, too. Many of them had moved at least once before. For example, the Robert Wilson Morrison family of Missouri was part of the Great Migration of 1843. Before going to Oregon, the Morrisons had moved three times since their marriage in 1831. Martha Gay of Springfield, Missouri, traveled the Oregon Trail with her parents, brothers, and sisters in 1851, when she was fourteen years old. The Gay family had already moved five times, to Kentucky, Tennessee, Arkansas, and Missouri.

These emigrants knew what it was like to pack up their belongings and travel to a new home. They had learned how to clear land, plant fields, and build houses. Some of them had grown to love the wandering life. Henry Sager, who emigrated in 1844, was described by his daughter Catherine as "one of those restless men who are not content to remain long in one place."[1]

It was men, for the most part, who caught the "Oregon fever." Husbands and fathers were the ones who decided to move their families from place to place. Wives, daughters, and sisters often longed to put down roots and stay in one place, but they had to move on when their menfolk were ready to move.

Letters and diaries written by many pioneer women tell us how the women dreaded the long and dangerous trip on the Oregon Trail. An emigrant woman named Mary Jones remembered that in the winter of 1846, her husband had read a book about California. He "was carried away with the idea" of going west. Mary begged, "Oh, let us not go."[2] But Mary's husband was determined to emigrate, and she had to go along with his plans.

Some women agreed to emigrate, because they feared that their husbands would leave without them if they said no. Nancy Kelsey, a seventeen-year-old bride, was one of the first white women to travel overland to California. She was afraid of the trip—but she was more afraid of staying home and wondering what would happen to her husband if he went alone. She completed the journey carrying her baby in her arms, although she had to walk barefoot through the Sierra Nevadas after her shoes wore out.

Children, like wives, often wanted to stay home instead of setting out on the forbidding Oregon Trail. The eleven children in Martha Gay's family, for example, told their father that they wanted to stay in Springfield. "But children were expected to do as their parents said in those days," wrote Martha years later, "and father said we must come."[3]

The decision to emigrate also affected older family members. Grandparents knew that they might never again see children or grandchildren who took the Oregon Trail. The Western territories were far away, and most emigrants would never come back to the States to visit the relatives they had left behind. Rather than be separated from their loved ones forever, some older people decided to emigrate with them. A sick, elderly woman named Sarah Keyes set off on the Oregon Trail in 1846. Her son-in-law was taking his wife and children to California, and Keyes did not want to be separated from her daughter and her grandchildren. The trip was too difficult for Keyes, however, and she died along the way.

Emigrants sometimes gave keepsake photographs such as this to the friends and relatives they left behind. Photography was new, and photographs were expensive. This might be the only picture ever taken of these people.

Some elderly relatives could not even try to make the journey. Young Martha Gay recalled saying good-bye to her grandmother. "The saddest parting of all," she wrote, "was when my mother took leave of her aged and sorrowing mother, knowing full well that they would never meet again on earth."[4]

However, another grandmother, Tabitha Brown of Massachusetts, went to Oregon at the age of sixty-seven to be with her married daughter and married son, who were moving to Oregon with their families. Brown's journey was a terrible ordeal. Her party took the Applegate Trail, a shortcut through southern Oregon that had been opened by Jesse Applegate. The travelers became lost, were attacked by Native Americans, and ran out of food. Brown lost all her possessions and nearly starved, but she survived. She arrived in Oregon penniless except for a single coin she found in one of her gloves. She used the coin to buy needles and thread and started a sewing business. Brown eventually earned enough money to help found one of the oldest colleges in the West, Pacific University in Forest Grove, Oregon. In 1987, the Oregon legislature named Tabitha Brown the "mother of Oregon."

The big question for many emigrants was: Oregon or California? Why did some people choose Oregon while others chose California? From the earliest days of emigration, California was thought of as wilder and more dangerous. After all, California still belonged to Mexico, and no one knew whether American settlers there would be able to hold on to their land claims. Single men were said to prefer California, and so were outlaws, scoundrels, and adventurers. This was especially true after gold was discovered in the Sacramento Valley, kicking off the Gold Rush of 1849. Thousands of prospectors poured into California to seek their fortunes.

Oregon, on the other hand, seemed more respectable. Many of the earliest American emigrants to Oregon were missionaries, and some of the first buildings in the area were churches. The Oregon branch of the trail was called "the family trail," because families who wanted land, security, and order generally went to Oregon. People in Oregon joked about the place where the Oregon and California branches of the trail divided. They said a pile of shiny rocks marked the California branch, while a sign that said "To Oregon" marked the Oregon branch. Emigrants seeking gold and riches chose the California branch. Those who could read went to Oregon.

Young or old, married or single, bound for California or Oregon, emigrants had to prepare carefully for the journey on the Oregon and California Trail. Their first task was to gather information. How would they get to their destination? What should they take with them?

Some found answers to these questions in letters from earlier emigrants. Since the 1830s, people like Nathaniel Wyeth had been writing to family members and friends in the United States about the wonders of the Oregon country. Early emigrants to California also sent letters to folks back

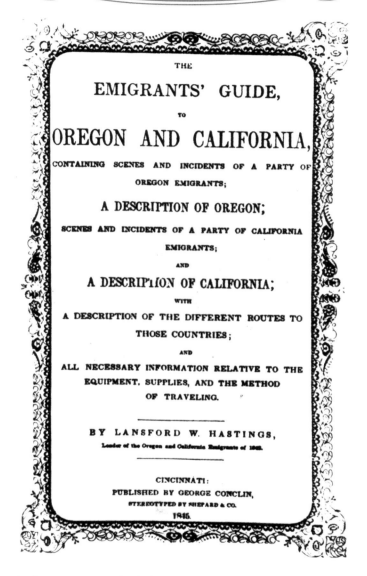

THE

EMIGRANTS' GUIDE,

TO

OREGON AND CALIFORNIA,

CONTAINING SCENES AND INCIDENTS OF A PARTY OF OREGON EMIGRANTS;

A DESCRIPTION OF OREGON;

SCENES AND INCIDENTS OF A PARTY OF CALIFORNIA EMIGRANTS;

AND

A DESCRIPTION OF CALIFORNIA;

WITH

A DESCRIPTION OF THE DIFFERENT ROUTES TO THOSE COUNTRIES;

AND

ALL NECESSARY INFORMATION RELATIVE TO THE EQUIPMENT, SUPPLIES, AND THE METHOD OF TRAVELING.

BY LANSFORD W. HASTINGS,

Leader of the Oregon and California Emigrants of 1842.

CINCINNATI:
PUBLISHED BY GEORGE CONCLIN,
STEREOTYPED BY SHEPARD & CO.
1845.

Lanford W. Hastings, who led a wagon train west in 1842, published this guidebook to the Oregon Trail. Unfortunately, some of the emigrants who followed Hastings's poor advice about a "shortcut" to California ended up lost and starving.

home. The letters were passed from hand to hand by hunters and trappers on the western trails until they reached the post offices of the Mississippi Valley, or they were carried around South America by ship. Those who received the letters read them eagerly and shared them with friends. Sometimes emigrants' letters were printed in the newspapers for all to see. The letters often explained where travelers could find grass and water for livestock along the trail, how they could get along with the Native Americans, and how to find the new settlements at the other end of the trail.

Guidebooks and handbooks for emigrants soon began to appear in bookstores. Some of these books were written by people who had traveled the Oregon Trail. They contained useful, accurate advice. Other guidebooks, however, were not worth the money emigrants paid for them. The authors of these worthless books had never traveled the routes they claimed to know. Unfortunately, emigrants could not always tell good advice from bad.

After choosing a destination and gathering information, emigrants had to collect the supplies and equipment they would need for the trip. The most important piece of equipment was the wagon. Movies and television programs often show emigrants riding west in large Conestoga wagons with swooping, curved white canopies, but this image is wrong for two reasons.

First, most emigrants on the Oregon Trail did not ride. They walked—all two thousand miles. Some men rode ahead on horseback to scout the route, but the rest traveled on foot, guiding their livestock. Women and children generally walked, too. The wagons were for carrying precious supplies, not passengers. Only the very old, the very young, the sick, and pregnant women rode in the wagons. Because the wagons had no springs, most emigrants found it more comfortable to walk than to be bounced around inside the wagons. Some emigrants did sleep in their wagons at night, but others slept in the open under canvas tents.

Second, most emigrants did not use Conestoga wagons, which were expensive and too wide and heavy for narrow mountain trails. They used smaller farm wagons with canvas tops stretched over hoops. The average wagon was about ten feet long and four feet wide. These wagons could carry loads of about twenty-five hundred pounds. A sturdy wagon was important. Emigrants could lose everything they owned if their wagon broke down along the way. The travelers carried spare wheels, buckets of axle grease to keep the wheels turning smoothly, and barrels of tar. They used the tar to waterproof the wagons so they could float the wagons across streams without ruining their contents.

Some families needed more than one wagon. Martha Gay's large family traveled west with four wagons. The Wilson family had two wagons for the seven Morrisons and John Minto, a single twenty-one-year-old who wanted to go west. Minto agreed to help Morrison care for his livestock, and in return Morrison provided food and shelter for Minto during the journey. Many of the single men who took the Oregon Trail traveled as the employees or companions of family groups.

Horses pulled some emigrant wagons. Most wagons, however, were pulled by oxen, which are sturdier than horses. The emigrants also knew that Native Americans along the route were less likely to steal oxen than horses. Each loaded wagon needed eight to ten oxen. Whenever possible, emigrants brought extra animals to replace oxen that died along the way. They also brought horses and cattle—and sometimes chickens, pigs, and dogs—for the homesteads they planned to start at the end of the trail.

Packing for the trip was no easy matter. One handbook said that each emigrant would need at least two-hundred pounds of flour, one-hundred fifty pounds of bacon, twenty pounds of sugar, and ten pounds each of salt and coffee for the Oregon Trail. Many travelers also carried dried fruits and vegetables. In addition, they relied on the wagon train's hunters to supply fresh meat, and they traded with the Native Americans they met along the way for vegetables, meat, and fish.

It cost between $500 and $1,000 to equip a family for the journey, depending upon the size of the family and its style of travel. Some emigrants scraped by with old, broken-down wagons, tired oxen, and the bare minimum of food, while a few wealthier folks traveled grandly in custom-built wagons. Many of the families who went west had to save for several years to pay for the trip.

The emigrants carried with them not only supplies for the journey but also the goods they would need to set up their new homes. They took seeds and a plow so they could plant crops, tools so they could fell trees and build a house, and spinning wheels and looms so they could make cloth. They also carried items that might be expensive or hard to obtain in the Western territories: blankets, shoes, lanterns, needles, thread, mirrors, matches, writing paper and pens, and medicines.

Here is what the Morrisons took in their two wagons to feed eight people on the trail and to start a new homestead in Oregon: one thousand pounds of flour, a large box of cornmeal, seven bags of beans, several hundred pounds each of bacon and sugar, a bag of dried apples and one of dried peaches, a keg of honey, clothing, bedding, a tent, cooking utensils, the iron parts of a plow, several types of seeds, a spinning wheel, and four rifles.

At the start of the trail, many of the emigrant wagons carried furniture—perhaps a rocking chair or a chest of drawers. Sadly, these prized possessions often had to be abandoned if the oxen became too weak to pull a heavy load. The road west was lined with furniture, trunks of books and china, and other items that travelers had been forced to abandon. One eleven-year-old girl never forgot a man named Smith who traveled west in her family's wagon train. When the men of the wagon train decided that everyone had to throw away all unnecessary items to lighten the wagon loads, Smith stood and wept as he

This print by artist Theodore R. Davis shows horses being driven into a corral formed by the covered wagons of a wagon train. On the left, in the foreground, is a family gathered at the rear of the two wagons. The family's possessions fill every corner of the wagon. Some of these treasured objects might be discarded along the trail if the load became too heavy for the weary oxen.

held an old wooden rolling pin. "Do I have to throw this away?" he pleaded. "It was my mother's. I remember she always used it to roll out her biscuits, and they were awful good biscuits."[5]

Once the supplies were loaded into the wagon, the emigrants headed for Independence or another jumping-off place along the Missouri River. There they waited until the time was right to begin the journey. Emigrants had to wait until the spring snows were gone from the prairies and the western plains had enough grass to feed the livestock. But they dared not wait too long, for they had to reach the far end of the trail before the snow began to fall.

Most of the wagon trains left in May. The emigrants set out with flags waving and spirits high, hoping to reach Oregon or California by October. In 1850, when fifteen-year-old Rebecca Nutting's family set out for California, Rebecca was excited about the trip ahead. She wrote in her diary, "Oh, we were going to have just a happy time."[6]

5

LIFE ON THE ROAD

No one wanted to travel the Oregon Trail alone. It was much safer and easier to travel in groups. Some small wagon trains consisted of people who had known each other for years—relatives or neighbors who decided to go west together. Other, larger wagon trains formed when emigrants gathered in the jumping-off places and agreed to travel together. Some of the biggest wagon trains had several hundred wagons and huge livestock herds.

The first task for the members of a wagon train was to get organized. The men in the group elected a leader, or captain. The emigrants usually wrote up a set of rules, too. Everyone who was part of the wagon train agreed to follow these rules. The captain's job was to make sure these rules were obeyed. Sometimes the emigrants also hired an experienced pilot who would start the train in motion every day and choose a campsite every night.

The emigrants were leaving the United States and its laws behind, so they set their own punishments for crimes, such as fighting or stealing supplies. They even held their own courts on the road. One group, after finding a man guilty of stealing something from another's wagon, sentenced him to be tied to the ground in the hot sun for a certain number of hours. In another wagon train, a man who killed another man in a knife fight was banished from the train. He was forced to ride off alone on horseback, leaving his wife and children with the group. He completed the journey on his own, however, and was reunited with his family in California.

Sometimes organizing a wagon train turned out to be more complicated than anyone had expected. In 1844, the emigrants of one wagon train spent four days camped on the prairie, arguing over who was to be the leader and how he should run things. Another wagon train produced a very complicated system of government, with a written constitution and a dozen elected officials. These officials felt that they should be excused from standing guard at night, and before the trip was over, the rest of the emigrants grew disgusted with their laziness and scrapped the whole constitution. But most wagon trains managed to get along fairly well, although people tended to grumble about their leaders when the going got difficult.

It did not take long for the emigrants to fall into the rhythm of wagon-train life—the rhythm of sunrise and sunset. No one wanted to waste time; everyone wanted the wagons to cover as many miles as possible each day.

The emigrants got their wagons rolling by seven each morning, and by eight at night they had finished their evening meal and were getting ready to sleep.

Everyone had plenty of work to do each day. A few men in each party served as scouts and hunters. These scouts rode far in front of the wagons. They kept the wagon train on track, steering by landmarks, and they warned the leader of any problems ahead, such as a band of hostile Native Americans or a flooded creek. The hunters rode out for fifteen miles or so on either side of the wagon train, looking for deer, antelope, or buffalo for the evening meal. The rest of the men traveled with the wagon train. Some of them guided the oxen, while others walked behind, herding the horses and cattle. The men of the wagon train also took turns standing guard at night.

Women worked extremely hard on the Oregon Trail. Most of the women who made the journey had children to care for. Many of them became pregnant or had babies while they were on the road. Childbirth on the trail was never easy. When water for washing was scarce, women had to do without clean sheets and baby clothes. Wagons offered little privacy for mothers in labor. Often there was no doctor on hand, so women helped one another through their troubles as best they could. Because emigrants always worried about falling behind schedule, a wagon train would usually pause for just one day while a woman gave birth. The next day she would be on her way again, enduring the heat and dust, and the jolting motion of the wagon over the rough trail.

In addition to caring for their children, women would cook for their families. Many women had never cooked over an open fire before, and they had to learn how to bake bread in a skillet and keep it from falling into the ashes. The women also mended torn clothing, washed their family's clothes and blankets when they could do so, packed and unpacked the wagons every day, and made the beds.

Children, too, were kept busy. Older girls helped their mothers with the sewing and cooking and took care of the younger children. Older boys helped their fathers herd the livestock. Sometimes teenage boys were allowed to join the hunters or to take turns as night watchmen. The boys considered it an honor to be chosen for these jobs. Even young children had work to do. They gathered buffalo chips for fuel, milked the cows, and kept the butter buckets full. The emigrants had learned that if they hung a bucket of milk on the wagon in the morning, by the end of the day the rocking and jolting of the wagon would have churned the milk into butter.

The emigrants' basic meal on the trail was bread, beans, and bacon for breakfast, lunch, and dinner— unless the hunters provided fresh meat to roast. Everyone drank coffee, even the children. The water from many of the springs and streams along the trail was bitter or dirty, and coffee disguised its bad taste. One emigrant's thirsty horse refused to drink the water at an especially bitter spring—but when the man used the water to make coffee, the horse drank the coffee.

Water polluted by human or animal waste could make the travelers sick. Among the worst illnesses spread this way was cholera, a deadly disease that struck many travelers on the Oregon Trail. The years 1849 and 1850 were especially bad; thousands of emigrants perished in cholera epidemics. Cholera is caused by bacteria that flourish in dirty water. In humans, these bacteria cause diarrhea, fever, vomiting, and death from severe dehydration. Death from cholera was painful and quick—victims usually died less than a dozen hours after the first signs of illness. Because nearly all cholera victims died, the members of wagon trains sometimes began digging graves as soon as people became sick.

Other diseases claimed victims along the trail. Smallpox, scarlet fever, and influenza were especially dangerous to newborns, young children, old people, and anyone else who was weak or tired. Accidents also killed or injured a good number of emigrants. Men and boys drowned while swimming their livestock across rivers. People were killed in hunting accidents or when a wagon slipped backward while they were pushing it up a hill. The saddest accidents involved children who fell from

Historians estimate that anywhere between ten thousand and thirty thousand people died along the Oregon Trail. These victims were remembered with monuments, but most were buried in unmarked graves.

wagons. When this happened, the children could be crushed by the heavy wheels before anyone could halt the wagon. The grave of little Joel Hembree can still be seen in east central Wyoming; he fell from a wagon in 1843.

One 1846 emigrant's journal recorded such a tragedy:

> Made an early start from the spring . . . but was stopped by an awful calamity. Mr. Collins's son George, about 6 years old, fell from the wagon and the wheels ran over his head, killing him instantly; the remainder of the day occupied in burying him.[1]

Ten-year-old Catherine Sager survived a fall from her wagon—although her left leg was crushed under the wagon's wheel. Sadly, Catherine's father was later killed by stampeding buffalo, and her mother fell sick and died.

Every wagon train had its share of deaths and funerals. In most places, wood was too scarce for the emigrants to build coffins. Instead, the travelers wrapped their dead in canvas, buried them, and piled rocks on the graves to keep animals from digging up the bodies. Sometimes the dead were buried in the trail itself, so the oxen and wagons would pack the earth firmly over the graves. Soon the sides of the trail were lined with grave markers, each one a simple monument to loss and sorrow. One morning while Francis Parkman was riding the trail, he saw a piece of wood standing upright on a small hill. He rode up the hill and found that these words had been burned into the board with a red-hot iron:

MARY ELLIS
DIED MAY 7TH, 1845
AGED TWO MONTHS[2]

Almost every letter or diary written by an emigrant tells of similar sights. Historians believe that at least 10 percent of all the emigrants died and were buried along the Oregon Trail.

But the trail had its bright side. Death may have stalked the emigrants, but they enjoyed life whenever they could. Especially during the early days, when travel across the prairies was uneventful and everyone felt strong, the trip sometimes felt like one long, joyous camping trip. In the evenings, the emigrants parked their wagons in a circle and ate their suppers. Sometimes they told stories, sang, and danced around their campfires. Anyone who had a fiddle or a harmonica was begged for a tune. People who had brought books offered to read them aloud. Children played hide-and-seek or tag among the wagons.

Fellowship and friendship helped ease the difficulties of the journey for many of the emigrants. Some of the friendships born on the trail lasted a lifetime. Often families that met in the wagon trains decided to settle

Following in the ruts made by hundreds of earlier wagons, a wagon train crosses a mountain pass in 1866. A traveler has painted his or her name on the large boulder at the side of the trail. Many emigrants took the time to mark their passage in this way.

near each other in the new territories. Young men and women met on the trail, flirted, courted—and perhaps were married, if there was a minister in the wagon train. Boys and girls who missed the friends they had left behind at home made new friends on the trail, for almost every wagon train had plenty of children. One emigrant who had made the crossing at the age of eight later remembered the journey as fun, saying, "We just had the time of our lives."[3]

6

DANGERS AND DISASTERS

The Oregon Trail was full of surprises that could cause trouble for the emigrants. Far from the nearest town or store or doctor, the emigrants had nowhere to turn for help in an emergency. The journey to the West brought them face to face with many new and unexpected dangers.

Even the weather could be a threat. As the wagon trains rolled along through the prairie grasses and flowers, the smiling blue skies could give way to a summer thunderstorm. The colossal storms of the plains terrified the emigrants with claps of thunder, sizzling blasts of lightning, roaring winds that ripped the canvas roofs from wagons, hailstones as big as a man's fist, and heavy rains that turned the trail into a sea of sticky mud.

"The whole sky became as black as ink," said one emigrant girl, describing a thunderstorm that struck her wagon train in 1846. "The rain came down in bucketfuls, drenching us to the skin. There wasn't a tent in camp that held against the terrific wind. The men had to chain the wagons together to keep them from being blown into the river."[1] Francis Parkman wrote that he had never seen or heard lightning and thunder like that he experienced on the Oregon Trail. An emigrant named Edward Parrish wrote, "It may be this was the heaviest fall of rain I ever experienced, or ever will."[2] Another grumbled, as he and his family hid from the lightning by crouching in the mud under their wagon, that he had never thought there was so much rain in the whole wide world.

Later in the journey, however, the emigrants looked back longingly on the rainstorms. Travelers bound for Oregon had to cross the barren desert of southeastern Oregon, while those headed for California had to cross even wider deserts in Utah and Nevada. Day after day, the wind whipped harsh sand and dust into the travelers' eyes. Many people who took the Oregon Trail suffered from lifelong eye problems brought on by the powdery dust.

In the barren, sun-dried deserts, every drop of water was precious. Travelers who depended upon finding springs or rivers sometimes went thirsty because they could not find water. Wagon-train leaders had to ration the water—for example, each person might be allowed one cup of water a day. In the desert heat, the emigrants soon became weak, dizzy, and ill from lack of water. Mothers gave their crying children smooth

Lightning strikes a lone tree during a thunderstorm in the Platte River country. Such storms could produce sudden floods. One wagon train was forced to wait for two weeks until a flooded creek grew calm enough to cross in safety.

pebbles to suck, hoping that this would ease the pangs of thirst. One woman wrote in her diary that she had "swallowed dust all day in place of water."[3]

The land itself sometimes seemed like an enemy. Creeks and rivers had to be crossed, and many emigrants lost livestock or supplies in these crossings. The hard ground rattled and shook the wagons; rocks splintered the hooves of the oxen. One woman who had crossed over the continent to California as a teenager later recalled that the oxen had often slipped and fallen on smooth, slippery rocks, leaving the rocks stained with blood from their knees. The farther west the emigrants went, the steeper and more rugged the trail became.

When the emigrants reached Fort Hall, they were three quarters of the way through their journey. They had only 550 more miles to go. But those final miles would be the hardest. The landscape was brutal, the emigrants and their oxen were tired, and supplies were running low.

California-bound emigrants headed off across the salt flats of Utah and Nevada, beyond which towered the Sierra Nevada range. Oregon-bound emigrants headed north for many miles along the Bear River and then west along the Snake River canyon. The late-summer heat beat down upon them as they trudged for mile after weary mile through a wilderness of dry boulders. Then came the Blue Mountains, a more difficult barrier than the much higher Rockies. Sometimes the emigrants were caught by early snowstorms in these bleak hills. Finally, after they came down out of the Blue Mountains, the weary travelers faced their last obstacle: the Columbia River. They loaded themselves and their goods into boats for the days-long journey through the river's powerful rapids.

Jesse Applegate, who helped lead the 120 wagons of the Great Migration to Oregon in 1843, was one of many who met disaster on the Columbia. The Applegate family and their goods filled two boats. A Native American guide they had hired rode in one of the boats. That boat made it safely through a dangerous stretch of rocky rapids, but the second boat was less lucky. It overturned, and three people were drowned. One was Applegate's young nephew, and one was his son Warren. The grief-stricken survivors made their way down the river to Fort Vancouver and the Willamette Valley.

Could emigrants reach the valley without risking their lives on the river? A lot of people dreamed of finding a better route across Oregon. One of them was Stephen Meek. He and his brother Joe were fur trappers who had settled in the Oregon country. The other settlers made Joe Meek Oregon's first sheriff in 1843. Stephen Meek became a guide and helped lead the 1842 emigrant party. In 1845, at Fort Boise on the Snake River, he met several hundred wagons and several thousand people bound for the Willamette Valley.

Stephen Meek offered to guide the emigrants on a cutoff. Meek said that his cutoff, an old Indian trail over the Blue and Cascade mountains, would bypass the deadly

Columbia River rapids. He promised that those who followed him would reach the valley weeks before those who took the slower river route. However, Meek had never actually seen this shortcut trail. He just believed that he could find it.

Some 250 pioneers agreed to try Meek's cutoff. He led them west into a rocky, mountainous, and dry landscape. The only water was in a few rivers that cut through deep canyons. Between rivers, the emigrants often went for days without finding water. Meek led his wagon train back and forth on a zigzag course, and soon the furious emigrants realized that he was as lost and confused as they were. They cursed him for deceiving them, and some of the men spoke of lynching him, but in the end, they all struggled on together. Every time they camped, they scattered in all directions, searching for a pond or a spring. One by one they began to die of starvation or from drinking the poisonous water that pooled in the salt flats.

Abandoning the idea of pushing westward across the Cascade Mountains, the desperate emigrants turned north, hoping to make it to the Dalles and the Columbia River. The survivors staggered into the Dalles late that autumn, forty days behind the emigrants who had taken the regular route. Seventy-five members of Meek's party had died, and Meek and his wife fled to escape the fury of those who lived.

The story of "Meek's Terrible Cutoff" lives on in Oregon legend. According to one version of the tale,

The Columbia River in Oregon as it appears today.

young emigrants out looking for water found some shiny stones, carried them back to the wagons in a blue bucket, and then forgot about them. Not until several years later did one of the young men realize that the stones were gold nuggets. He went back to central Oregon and searched and searched for the place he had found the nuggets, but he never found it. People today are still looking for the lost Blue Bucket Mine.

"Meek's Terrible Cutoff" was not the only cutoff that led emigrants into trouble. The next year, tragedy struck a group of Illinois emigrants bound for California who took a cutoff. The group, known as the Donner-Reed Party, had read a book called *The Emigrant's Guide to Oregon and California*. The author of the book was a man named Lansford W. Hastings, who wanted to start an independent republic in California. To encourage people to come to California, he described a shortcut south of the Great Salt Lake. Hastings claimed that this cutoff would make the trip to California quicker and easier than the usual emigrant route. Many hopeful emigrants bought Hastings's book. They did not know that Hastings had never seen the cutoff he described. He had only heard about it from trappers and Native Americans.

In July, the Donner-Reed Party, following Hastings's directions, veered south of the main Oregon Trail route. Unfortunately, the Hastings cutoff led them straight into some of the most rugged territory of the West: the Wasatch Mountains of northeastern Utah. It took the travelers weeks of agonizing labor to clear trees and boulders to make a wagon trail through the mountains. Often they came to steep bluffs or cliffs where they had to take their wagons apart and raise or lower them on chains. Then, after they made it through the mountains, the Donner-Reed Party had to cross the Great Salt Lake Desert. Hastings had promised that the desert crossing would take two days, but it took five. The emigrants' water ran out, and they went half crazy from thirst.

In October, the Donner-Reed Party rejoined the regular trail at the end of the Hastings cutoff. By this time, however, the emigrants were in serious trouble. They had been running late even before the "shortcut," and the cutoff had cost them weeks of precious time. The other wagons of the season had already passed through the steep Sierra Nevada range and were in the pleasant Sacramento Valley of California. But the Donner-Reed Party still had to make it across the Sierra pass. Tragically, they were just a few days too late. By the time they reached the pass, the snow of an early winter was too deep for them to get through. They spent the winter huddled in miserable, snowbound camps on the eastern side of the Sierras. Their food gave out, and they had to boil leather harness straps to make broth. Soon they began to sicken and die. By the time Californians came across the mountains to rescue the Donner-Reed Party in February, some of the starving emigrants had begun eating the flesh of their dead companions. Of the eighty-nine people in the group,

This photo was taken at Donner Lake in 1866. The stumps of trees cut down by the Donner-Reed Party were still there.

forty-two died. Some historians call the Donner-Reed Party the worst disaster in the whole westward migration.

Meanwhile, settlers in Oregon were busy improving their end of the Oregon Trail. The horrors of "Meek's Terrible Cutoff" showed the need for a safer route to the Willamette Valley. In 1846, two emigrants named Samuel Barlow and Joel Palmer discovered a route across the southern shoulder of Mount Hood and cleared a road. From that time on, emigrants who reached the Dalles had a choice: They could travel overland through the Cascades on the Barlow Road, or they could go by water down the Columbia. They had to pay to use the Barlow Road, but they also had to pay if they used Native American guides and canoes on the river.

The Barlow Road was safer than the river, but it was not easy. Parts of the road were dreadfully steep. The worst part of the road was a stretch called Laurel Hill. Here the men of the wagon train had to haul the wagons up the hill with chains or ropes and then lower them carefully down the other side. More than one wagon broke free to smash on the rocks below.

The Barlow Road was not the only new stretch of trail created in 1846. That year Applegate and several other settlers decided to open a route from Fort Hall into southern Oregon. They rode south from the Willamette Valley across the valleys of the Umpqua and Rogue rivers, and then across a corner of California to the Black Rock Desert of Nevada and Fort Hall. There

Modern paved roads make it easy to get through Donner Pass. Still at certain times of the year, the weather can make it a treacherous journey.

they persuaded a group of Oregon-bound emigrants to return with them over the same route, which came to be called the Applegate Trail.

The emigrants' first trip across the Applegate Trail was a disaster. They had a horribly difficult time getting their wagons across the knot of mountains on the California-Oregon border. They traveled so slowly that they ran out of food and were caught in the cold rains of an Oregon winter while they were still far from the Willamette Valley settlements. Furthermore, they were attacked several times by Native Americans who wanted to keep whites out of southern Oregon.

In spite of this dismal beginning, the Applegate Trail was later used by thousands of emigrants. In 1853, for example, more than thirty-five hundred men, women, and children came to Oregon by Applegate's route. After 1859, when gold was discovered along the Rogue River, prospectors and miners poured into southern Oregon on the Applegate Trail.

More than storms, hunger, or thirst, the pioneers of the Oregon Trail feared Native Americans. Emigrant James Clyman reported that most of those who went west in his wagon train expected to meet "the war whoop and the scalping knife."[5] One eighteen-year-old girl whose family planned to emigrate was warned that Native Americans would kill them all before they got to Oregon.

The wagon trains that brought white settlers to the West brought trouble for the Native Americans. Whites had already seized most of the land in the East, either killing the native peoples or forcing them to move to special territories. The same thing would eventually happen in the West and on the Great Plains. White settlers would outnumber the Native Americans, the U.S. government would negotiate treaties and then dishonor them, and white soldiers would overpower the Native Americans. First, however, many Native Americans fought to keep whites from taking over their territory. Warriors sometimes attacked emigrant wagon trains—the Umpqua, for example, attacked emigrants on the Applegate Trail.

Relations between settlers and Native Americans in Oregon country worsened after 1847. That year, the Cayuse of eastern Washington, believing that white people were spreading disease to Native American children, attacked the Whitman mission near Walla Walla and killed Marcus and Narcissa Whitman along with a dozen other whites. The Oregon settlers responded by forming a volunteer army to attack the Cayuse. For the next thirty years, fighting flared from time to time between white settlers and the Native American peoples of Washington, Oregon, and Idaho.

The great majority of travelers along the Oregon Trail had no trouble with Native Americans. Some emigrants never saw any of them at all. But many wagon trains had peaceful contacts with them. Native American women often came to the emigrants' camps with dried

A modern view of the rocky trail on Mount Hood.

meat or fish; vegetables; or moccasins, shoes made of hide. The emigrants were eager to trade needles, old clothing, or flour for these useful items. More often than not, it was the emigrant women who did the trading. Their fear of the Native Americans faded a bit after a few friendly meetings. Native Americans also guided some wagon trains over parts of the trail, showed emigrants where to find water, and ferried travelers and their wagons across rivers.

A few emigrants did have terrifying encounters with fierce Native Americans. But many shared the experience of Amelia Stewart Knight, who crossed the plains in 1853. "I lay awake all night," she wrote in her diary after sighting Native Americans. "I expected we would all be killed. However, we all found our scalps on in the morning."[7] Like Knight, a number of emigrants found that their fears were unfounded. Many more pioneers were killed by accident or disease than by the arrows and tomahawks of the Native Americans.

7

THE END OF
THE TRAIL

When they reached the end of the trail, what did the emigrants find in Oregon? An emigrant named B. F. Nichols was happy with what he found. To him, the Willamette Valley was "an earthly paradise" with "grass 12 to 15 inches high and green all winter."[1] Another emigrant, who arrived in 1845 said, "The whole country was a natural park."[2]

Some emigrants, however, were a little disappointed in Oregon. Life was hard there, especially in the early years. The Willamette Valley settlements were small and primitive. Clearing the land of its enormous trees was a back-breaking task.

To make matters worse, emigrants generally arrived in Oregon in the fall. They were bone-tired, but they were also eager to start their new lives. Yet it was difficult to clear land and build houses during the winter. Elizabeth Dixon Smith, her husband, and their eight children traveled the Oregon Trail in 1847, making the last stretch of the trip by water on the Columbia. In November, they arrived at the small, crude settlement that later became the city of Portland. Smith was not impressed. She wrote home that the only shelter her family could find was a shack, "a small leaky concern with 2 families already in it. You could have stirred us with a stick."[3]

Many newly arrived emigrants rushed to stake out their land claims, only to spend months camping in their wagons or tents before they could begin working the land. Those who had lost their wagons or their possessions during the trip were in terrible trouble. Fortunately, many emigrants had friends or relatives in the Oregon country. One historian believes that nearly half the settlers in Oregon in the 1840s and 1850s had family members already settled there. People without wagons or tents could find temporary homes with relatives. The spirit of fellowship that most emigrants shared on the trail remained alive in the new settlements. People generally offered a helping hand to anyone who needed it. Settlers who were well established in Oregon remembered their own troubles on the trail and were generous to new arrivals.

There was little money in Oregon in the early days. People bartered for what they needed, made it themselves, or did without. Years later, one man told how he had paid for an important purchase: "I packed butter in boxes on a pack 60 miles to pay for my wife's wedding dress."[4] Farmers used wheat as money. A bushel of wheat equaled one dollar.

Even people who had money could not always find things to buy with it. Goods reached the Oregon country by ship, but many items were in short supply. When Martha Ann Morrison reached Oregon in 1845, she desperately wanted new shoes and stockings to replace the ones that had worn out on the trail, but there were no shoes or stockings to buy. She also wanted cloth to make a dress, but there was only one bolt of calico in all of Oregon.

The year after she arrived in Oregon, fifteen-year-old Martha married John Minto, who had worked his way west by tending her family's livestock along the trail. They set up housekeeping near Salem, but they could not find a stove to buy. They had one kettle for boiling coffee, baking bread, and frying meat. The young couple also had two plates and three knives—but they could not get spoons or forks for three or four years. Martha was a tough and resourceful young woman, however. She was only sixteen when her husband went off to fight in one of the Indian wars, but she managed to drive off the wolves that came every night to threaten the Mintos' livestock.

Another problem for some emigrants was the weather. Oregon winters were not terribly cold, but they were wet. Some emigrants thought that it would never stop raining. Thirteen-year-old Martha Washburn will never forgot her first winter in Oregon. She remembered "the weeping skies and my mother also weeping."[5]

Still, the emigrants kept coming. Each year after the Great Migration of 1843, several thousand people took the Oregon Trail to Oregon or California. The number leaped to twenty-five thousand in 1849 and fifty thousand in 1850, although most of those travelers were bound for the gold fields of California, not for Oregon.

These years brought many changes to California and Oregon. California and the Southwest became a U.S. territory in 1848, after the United States fought a war with Mexico. In 1850, California became a state.

American settlers in Oregon were hungry for statehood as well. The United States and Great Britain had shared the Oregon country since 1818. Once the wagon trains began rolling west, however, the American settlers greatly outnumbered the British in the region. These Americans wanted to be part of the United States. As early as 1838, missionary Jason Lee carried a letter to Washington, D.C., asking the federal government to take charge of Oregon.

In 1846, Great Britain and the United States agreed to divide the Oregon country. Great Britain took the northern part, which is now the province of British Columbia, Canada. The United States received the southern part, which now makes up the states of Washington, Idaho, and Oregon. This region was called the Oregon Territory. Congress invited Abraham Lincoln, who had served four terms in the Illinois state legislature and was on the verge of entering national politics, to be the territory's first governor. Lincoln turned down the offer, and Congress appointed General Joseph Lane instead.

The Oregon Territory grew rapidly during the 1850s. New towns sprang up along the Willamette River, on the rolling plains of central Oregon near the fast-growing community called the Dalles, in the hills and valleys of southern Oregon along the Applegate Trail, and on the coast. Roads linked these settlements, and the Willamette was busy with river traffic. Settlers replaced their first crude log cabins with plank houses. The wild landscape gave way to schools, churches, fences, stores, cemeteries, and other signs of settled life. In 1853, the Oregon Territory was divided into two smaller territories, Oregon and Washington. The Idaho Territory was separated from Washington in 1863. Oregon, which attracted most of the settlers in the early years of emigration, became a state in 1859; Washington would follow in 1889, and Idaho in 1890.

The tide of settlers continued to flow along the Oregon Trail. In the eleven years from 1849 to 1860, nearly three hundred thousand people crossed the plains: two hundred thousand to California, fifty-three thousand to Oregon, and forty-three thousand to Salt Lake City in Utah. The tide slowed a bit in the years 1861–65, when the United States was torn by the Civil War, although some men went west to escape being drafted, and many

Southerners headed west when the South began to lose the war. When the Civil War ended, the westward emigration again picked up strength. Each year, a few thousand emigrant wagons creaked and rumbled along the Oregon Trail.

But the trail was changing. By this time, there was a bridge across the North Platte River, where the first emigrants had struggled to free their wagons from the quicksand. Other streams and creeks had been bridged, too, and government engineers had used dynamite to flatten hills and widen narrow places along the road.

In the early days there had been one trail, with a California branch and an Oregon branch, and then the Applegate branch between the two. By the 1860s, though, there were many trails. Emigrants were branching off the main routes, creating side trails and new cutoffs. People were beginning to settle the Rocky Mountains and the Great Plains. Gold strikes in Colorado and Nevada in 1859 lured many miners to those regions, and a gold strike in Idaho in 1860 did the same thing, making people turn off the trail to found new communities in Idaho. The Oregon Trail was no longer a single highway leading to the West Coast. Instead it was the center of a fast-growing network of roads and trails that spread across the land west of the Missouri River.

Emigrants were no longer the only ones who traveled the Oregon Trail. By the 1860s, freight companies had begun shipping goods westward in wagon caravans on the trail. The Central Overland California and Pike's Peak

Gold strikes in Colorado and Nevada in 1859 similar to the one in California lured many miners to these regions. These miners are using equipment from a typical prospecting kit, including a pan, a pick and an all-purpose shovel. When two or three miners worked together, they often used a "rocker" —a boxlike, wooden device for "washing" larger quantities of dirt.

Express Company of Kansas, for example, operated more than six thousand wagons throughout the West, many of them on the Oregon Trail.

In 1863, the Central Pacific railroad company started building a railway line east from California. Two years later, the Union Pacific started building a line west from Omaha, Nebraska. The two lines met in Utah in 1869, and the first railway line across North America was complete. Soon goods and passengers could travel from the Missouri to the Oregon country in just a few days.

The railroads did not kill the Oregon Trail at once. Many emigrants could not afford to ship their families and their possessions west by train. In addition, farmers knew that they would need their livestock and wagons in the new settlements. So the wagon trains continued to roll west, slower than the railroad trains but steady and determined. James Kyner, who worked on railroads in the West during the 1880s, described a wagon train he saw heading west across Nebraska. "I could see an almost unbroken stream of emigrants from horizon to horizon," he wrote. "Teams and covered wagons . . . an endless stream of hardy, optimistic folk going west to seek their fortunes and to settle an empire."[6]

But the railroads did mark the beginning of the end for the Oregon Trail. The West was filling up and being tamed. Settlers now had to pay taxes and obey laws, just like everyone else in the United States. The

Railroad officials celebrate their railway's progress through Nebraska in 1866. Soon trains would cross the continent—but the railroads did not entirely replace the covered wagon and the Oregon Trail.

most desirable pieces of land had already been claimed. The westward migration began to taper off in the 1880s.

In 1893, Robert D. Porter, the head of the U.S. Census Bureau, made an important announcement. Porter had studied maps and reports of settlement from all over the country, and he had discovered that the frontier—the border between settled territory and wild land—no longer existed. "Up to and including 1880 the country had a frontier of settlement," Porter said, "but at present the unsettled area has been so broken into by isolated bodies of settlement, that there can hardly be said to be a frontier line."[7]

America had been settled from sea to shining sea. Plenty of wild, empty places still remained between settlements, but there was no longer a true frontier. The big wagon trains no longer rolled toward the setting sun. The glory days of the Oregon Trail were over.

8

THE OREGON TRAIL TODAY

The frontier died in 1893, and for a while it seemed that the Oregon Trail would die, too. But the Oregon Trail lives on in several ways. One of those ways is the modern cross-country highway system of the United States.

Emigrants and their wagons no longer stretch across the continent in a long line marching steadily westward, but people still travel west. Some of the roads they follow lead them along the old Oregon Trail. Today you can ride in air-conditioned cars on modern highways where the emigrants once walked beside their oxen, sweating in the summer heat.

In Nebraska, between the towns of Lowell and Brule, U.S. Highways 30 and 80 follow the route taken by the emigrants on the Oregon Trail. These highways run next to the Platte River. Although the emigrants complained that the Platte was "too dirty to bathe in and too thick to drink," they drank its water and grazed their livestock along its banks for hundreds of miles. West of Brule, Highway 26 follows the Oregon Trail route from Nebraska into Wyoming. It passes Fort Laramie, the trading post where so many of the emigrants stopped to rest their weary oxen and stock up on supplies.

In Wyoming, Highway 28 runs near the wagon road over the South Pass of the Rocky Mountains. This highway also carries today's travelers near an area that the emigrants called the "Parting of the Ways"—a region just west of South Pass where many of the emigrants took a shortcut called the Sublette Cutoff.

Farther west, in Idaho, Highways 86 and 84 pick up the trail at American Falls and follow it west along the Snake River for many miles. At Glenn's Ferry, though, the highways veer away from the route followed by most of the emigrants, who used the Snake River canyon as their guide through the wilderness. Highway 84 meets the old trail route again on the border between Idaho and Oregon and follows the trail through the Blue Mountains. Where emigrants once cursed and prayed and labored to get their wagons up and down steep, wooded slopes, today's tourists marvel at the magnificent scenery of this corner of Oregon.

From the Dalles, drivers can take Highway 84 west through the Columbia River gorge to Portland, Oregon, and Vancouver, Washington. On their right flows the broad blue Columbia, no longer the wild river of rapids and waterfalls that terrified the emigrants. Modern

Historic Fort Laramie as it appears today.

dams have tamed the Columbia and turned it into a placid shipping channel. If drivers want to see part of the old Barlow Road through the Cascade Mountains, they can take Highway 197 south and Highway 26 west around Mount Hood. Like the emigrants of old, they will come down from the mountain pass into the gentle, smiling Willamette Valley.

Many stretches of the California portion of the trail, too, can be traveled on modern roads. Highway 80 crosses over the Wasatch Mountains of Utah and loops south around the Great Salt Lake—the same route that caused so much trouble for the ill-fated Donner-Reed Party. Through Nevada, Highway 80 follows the route taken by thousands of California emigrants, heading west to Lake Tahoe. With its shores dotted with resorts, close to the cities of Reno and Carson City, Lake Tahoe today is a lively spot. A century and a half ago, though, it was a lonely resting place for the Donner-Reed Party and all the other emigrants who camped there, building up their strength for the last grueling climb up the Sierra Nevada range. Highway 80 follows the emigrant route up over the Sierra pass and down to Sacramento. Along the way, it passes Donner Memorial State Park, built on the area of land where the Donner-Reed Party spent their terrible winter.

Modern highways can carry us across the country where the emigrants traveled, but they are not the same thing as the Oregon Trail. Yet parts of the original trail still exist—thanks to one man.

A view of Donner Memorial State Park.

That man was Ezra Meeker, who traveled the Oregon Trail in 1852, at the age of twenty-two. Meeker settled in Oregon and watched the territory grow into a state. He saw pioneers growing older and dying, and he saw young people being born and growing up without knowing what it meant to cross a continent on foot. As the nineteenth century ended and the twentieth century began, Meeker began to fear that Americans in the age of automobiles and streetlights would forget how the emigrants had lived and died on the way west.

Meeker also saw that great stretches of the trail were being lost, in Oregon and in other places. Farmers plowed up the old wagon ruts to plant crops. Engineers built dams that flooded stretches of the trail or covered the trail with paved roads. Meeker decided to save what was left of the Oregon Trail before it was too late.

In 1906, Meeker was seventy-six years old and full of energy. That year, exactly one hundred years after Meriweather Lewis and William Clark returned from their historic expedition, Meeker set out with some oxen and a covered wagon to travel the Oregon Trail again. This time, however, he traveled from west to east—from Oregon to Missouri. Along the way, he stopped at hundreds of places that were part of the trail's history. Meeker's trip was a public occasion—he used every means he could think of to get publicity. By the time he arrived in a town, every newspaper editor, schoolteacher, and civic leader had

Ezra Meeker (on the left) in Baker City, Oregon, in 1906. Meeker, who came west in 1852, spent years encouraging the American people to preserve the Oregon Trail and its heritage. This granite monument is one of the many that Meeker's supporters placed along the trail.

received a letter from him announcing his visit and talking about preserving the Oregon Trail.

Meeker hoped that his cross-country trip would do three things. First, he wanted to retrace the route and identify places associated with the trail. He urged emigrants and the children of emigrants to meet him and tell their stories, and he asked cities and towns and counties to put up signs or monuments to mark important spots along the trail. Second, Meeker wanted to call the public's attention to how much of the trail and its history had already been lost. Third, and most important, he hoped to get Americans excited about the Oregon Trail. The trail was part of America's heritage, and he wanted them to learn about it and preserve it.

As part of his publicity campaign, Meeker wrote a book about his 1852 experiences on the Oregon Trail. He published it himself and used the money he earned by selling it to raise more publicity for the trail. Meeker's efforts continued. He made several other trips along the trail, one of them in an automobile. He also met with Presidents Theodore Roosevelt and Calvin Coolidge, urging them to protect the trail, and he spoke to the U.S. Congress about the importance of preserving the emigrant heritage.

In 1926, the ninety-six-year-old Meeker founded the Oregon Trail Memorial Association (OTMA) to promote the preservation of the trail. Meeker died two years later, but the OTMA carried on his work. Its first secretary was William Henry Jackson, an artist and photographer who had become famous for his pictures of the Western frontier. Jackson continued to win support for Meeker's dream.

In 1978, the U.S. Congress named the 2,170-mile-long Oregon Trail a National Historic Trail. The National Park Service, which is part of the Department of the Interior, is in charge of maintaining the trail. This does not mean that the entire trail is a national park. Much of the original trail is now on privately owned land. But the Park Service has identified 125 historic sites along the trail. It has also found seven cross-country stretches of the trail, totalling 318 miles, that have changed little since the emigrants crossed them. Twenty-eight of the historic sites and one-hundred ninety miles of the cross-country segments are on public land. Anyone can visit these places. In many spots visitors will see ruts carved deep in soil and rock by thousands of iron-bound wagon wheels.

The National Historic Trail begins on the banks of the Missouri River, north of Independence, Missouri. It travels to the National Frontier Trails Center in Independence, where a museum features exhibits about the Oregon and California Trail. Emigrants tell their own stories of triumph and tragedy through readings from their diaries and letters, and display cases contain clothes, tools, and other objects carried on the Oregon Trail. The museum is also the home of a research library containing material about the settling of the West.

Two rock formations in western Nebraska are part of Oregon Trail history. One is Chimney Rock. Emigrants along the trail saw that wind and rain were eroding the tall, thin spire of Chimney Rock, and many predicted that in fifty years the spire would disappear completely. They were wrong, however, and Chimney Rock still rises gracefully above the plain. It is now a National Historic Site. Thirty-five miles west is Scotts Bluff, a tall, steep hill that was another landmark for the emigrants. Scotts Bluff is a National Historic Monument. There, visitors can see wagon ruts that are several feet deep. The visitor center contains many of William Henry Jackson's drawings and watercolor paintings of scenes along the Oregon Trail.

Fort Laramie, in eastern Wyoming, has been preserved as a National Historic Site. Several of the original buildings are still standing. One of them, called "Old Bedlam," is the oldest building in Wyoming. A few miles west of the fort is Register Rock, one of many large rocks along the trail where emigrants carved or painted their names. Several hundred of these names can still be seen. Nearby are some of the best-preserved wagon ruts on the trail: five feet deep in sandstone.

Independence Rock, many miles west along the trail but still in Wyoming, is now a State Historic Site. Legend says that the rock was named by fur trappers who held a celebration there in 1824 on July 4, Independence Day. In later years, emigrants on the trail judged their progress by whether they had reached Independence Rock by July 4. If not, they were running late. They then had to speed up their pace or risk being snowbound in the mountains. Like Register Rock, Independence Rock was a place where thousands of emigrants signed their names. Some of them can still be read; time and vandals have destroyed the rest.

South Pass, where the Oregon Trail crossed the continental divide, has a number of historic markers. One of them was placed by Meeker in 1906 in honor of Narcissa Whitman and Eliza Spalding, the first white women to emigrate to the Oregon Territory. Other markers guide visitors to several Parting of the Ways sites.

Fort Hall, in Idaho, stood on a site that is now part of the Shoshone-Bannock reservation north of the city of Pocatello. A long stretch of wagon ruts crosses this reservation, but the original fort is gone. A replica of the fort has been built in Pocatello. West of there, the trail crosses the Raft River—the last place where emigrants could turn south for California. From here, the Oregon Trail began heading northwest along the Snake River.

Near Baker City, Oregon, where the trail began to ease up into the Blue Mountains, the Bureau of Land Management operates an Oregon Trail Interpretive Center. Opened in 1992, the center offers a detailed look at the emigrant experience through movies, guided walks, plays and shows, and interactive exhibits. The Oregon Trail lives on in the place names of the region—

Near Baker City, Oregon, where the trail began to ease up into the Blue Mountains, the Bureau of Land Management operates an Oregon Trail Interpretive Center. A reconstructed covered wagon sits in the center of this photograph with the Blue Mountains in the background.

such names as Emigrant Spring, Deadman Pass, and Fourmile Canyon. In Washington, just across the Columbia River, the old Whitman Mission is a National Historic Site. Once the scene of a tragic massacre, it is now a peaceful picnic area.

The Oregon Trail ended in the Willamette Valley. Emigrants who came down the Columbia River passed Fort Vancouver, which has been reconstructed in Vancouver, Washington, as a National Historic Site. Then they turned south up the Willamette River to Oregon City. Those who came across the Barlow Road over Mount Hood emerged at Oregon City, the original center of settlement in the valley. Today, the End of the Oregon Trail Interpretive Center in Oregon City, decorated with giant replicas of covered wagons, is a valuable source of information for anyone interested in the history of the Oregon Trail. Visitors to the center can look at real emigrant wagons and marvel at how the emigrants managed to carry so many things in such tiny wagons.

Many of the emigrants started their journey in Independence, and that Missouri town has not forgotten its connection to Oregon. When severe floods in February 1996 damaged the End of the Oregon Trail Center in Oregon City, schoolteachers in Independence raised money to help the center make repairs—proving that the spirit of pioneer fellowship can still reach from one end of the Oregon Trail to the other.

The National Park service operates a reconstruction of Fort Vancouver.
Shown here is one of the interior buildings. Dr. McLoughlin welcomed
the first emigrants to Oregon country and let them rest at the fort.

Today communities all along the trail celebrate the emigrant heritage with pageants, festivals, and reenactments of the crossing. The route is dotted with museums, visitor centers, and historic markers. The Oregon Trail has not been forgotten; old Meeker would be proud.

But facts and figures, dates, and places are not the important things to remember about the Oregon Trail. The important things are the human stories: the children who left their homes to face a great unknown; the women who coped with cooking and childbirth amid the rugged conditions of the trail; the men who took their families through months of toil and trouble, because they believed that life would be better for everyone at the other end of the trail. Some of those who walked the Oregon Trail were heroes, and some were cowards or fools. Most of them, though, were simply ordinary people doing their best in extraordinary times. They did more than just survive a journey. They created the American West.

1542—Spanish explorers are first Europeans to see Oregon coast.

1787—Robert Gray of Boston makes first American landing on Oregon coast.

1792—Gray gives Columbia River its name.

1803—In Louisiana Purchase, Thomas Jefferson buys central North America from France.

1804—Meriwether Lewis and William Clark lead first expedition from Mississippi River to Oregon coast and back.

1811—John Jacob Astor sets up fur-trading post in Oregon.

1812—Robert Stuart discovers South Pass through Rocky Mountains.

1818—United States and Great Britain agree to share Oregon country.

1824—Dr. John McLoughlin takes charge of Fort Vancouver, British trading post.

1830s—American emigrants and missionaries go to Oregon country.

1841—First organized wagon train to Oregon and California.

1842—John C. Frémont makes accurate maps of the West.

1843—The Great Migration—the first large wagon train to Oregon.

1846—United States and Great Britain divide Oregon country; Applegate Trail and Barlow Road open.

1847—Cayuse attack Whitman Mission near Walla Walla, Washington.

1848—United States takes California and the Southwest from Mexico.

1849—Gold Rush to California begins.

1850—California becomes a state.

1853—Washington Territory created from northern part of Oregon Territory.

1859—Oregon becomes a state.

1869—First railroad across United States completed.

1893—U.S. census director declares the frontier closed.

1906—Ezra Meeker begins campaign to preserve Oregon Trail.

1978—Congress establishes Oregon National Historic Trail.

1995—Congress establishes California National Historic Trail.

CHAPTER NOTES

Chapter 1 "Oregon Fever"

1. Irene M. Franck and David M. Brownstone, *To the Ends of the Earth: The Great Travel and Trade Routes of Human History* (New York: Facts on File, 1984), p. 298.

2. Martha Gay Masterson, *One Woman's West*, ed. Lois Barton (Eugene, Oreg.: Spencer Butte Press, 1990), p. 23.

3. Lillian Schlissel, *Women's Diaries of the Westward Journey* (New York: Schocken Books, 1982), p. 20.

Chapter 2 Looking Westward

1. Terence O'Donnell, *That Balance So Rare: The Story of Oregon* (Portland: Oregon History Society Press, 1988), p. 16.

Chapter 3 The Great Migration Begins

1. Francis Parkman, *The Oregon Trail*, ed. E. N. Feltskog (Madison: University of Wisconsin Press, 1969), p. 42.

2. Ibid., p. 66.

3. John Bidwell, Hubert Howe Bancroft, and James Longmire, *First Three Wagon Trains* (Portland: Binfords & Mort, n.d.), pp. 23–24.

4. Ibid., p. 9.

Chapter 4 Getting Started

1. Quoted in Sanford Wexler, *Westward Expansion: An Eyewitness History* (New York: Facts on File, 1991), p. 155.

2. Thomas A. Rumer, *The Wagon Trains of '44* (Spokane, Wash.: Arthur H. Clark, Co., 1989), p. 51.

3. Lillian Schlissel, *Women's Diaries of the Westward Journey* (New York: Schocken Books, 1982), p. 28.

4. Martha Gay Masterson, *One Woman's West*, ed. Lois Barton (Eugene, Oreg.: Spencer Butte Press, 1990), p. 23.

5. Ibid., p. 28.

6. Susan G. Butrille, *Women's Voices From the Oregon Trail* (Boise, Idaho: Tamarack Books, 1993), p. 21.

7. Schlissel, p. 234.

Chapter 5 Life on the Road

1. Brown and Pringle families genealogical volume at Pacific University, Forest Grove, Oregon. Quoted in Rebecca Stefoff, *Women Pioneers* (New York: Facts on File, 1995), p. 32.

2. Francis Parkman, *The Oregon Trail*, ed. E. N. Feltskog (Madison: University of Wisconsin Press, 1969), p. 56.

3. Lillian Schlissel, *Women's Diaries of the Westward Journey* (New York: Schocken Books, 1982), p. 8.

Chapter 6 Dangers and Disasters

1. Susan G. Butrille, *Women's Voices From the Oregon Trail* (Boise, Idaho: Tamarack Books, 1993), p. 23.

2. Thomas A. Rumer, *The Wagon Trains of '44* (Spokane, Wash.: Arthur H. Clark, Co., 1989), p. 202.

3. Quoted in Sanford Wexler, *Westward Expansion: An Eyewitness History* (New York: Facts on File, 1991), p. 173.

4. *The Pioneers* (Alexandria, Va.: Time-Life Books, 1974), p. 105.

5. In David Colbert, ed., *Eyewitness to America: 500 Years of America in the Words of Those Who Saw It Happen* (New York: Pantheon Books, 1997), p. 170.

6. Rumer, p. 225.

7. Lillian Schlissel, *Women's Diaries of the Westward Journey* (New York: Schocken Books, 1982), p. 209.

Chapter 7 The End of the Trail

1. Thomas A. Rumer, *The Wagon Trains of '44* (Spokane, Wash.: Arthur H. Clark Co., 1989), p. 241.

2. Ibid., p. 242.

3. Susan G. Butrille, *Women's Voices From the Oregon Trail* (Boise, Idaho: Tamarack Books, 1993), p. 124.

4. Rumer, p. 241.

5. Butrille, p. 121.

6. Jay Monaghan, *The Book of the American West* (New York: Messner, 1963), p. 111.

7. Sanford Wexler, *Westward Expansion: An Eyewitness History* (New York: Facts on File, 1991), p. 301.

FURTHER READING

Domnauer, Teresa. *Westward Expansion*. New York: Children's Press, 2010.

——. *Life in the West*. New York: Children's Press, 2010.

Harness, Cheryl. *The Tragic Tale of Narcissa Whitman and a Faithful History of the Oregon Trail*. Washington, D.C.: National Geographic Society, 2006.

Huey, Lois Miner. *American Archaeology Uncovers the Westward Movement*. New York: Marshall Cavendish Benchmark, 2010.

Klausmeyer, David. *Oregon Trail Stories: True Accounts of Life in a Covered Wagon*. Guilford, Conn.: TwoDot, 2004.

McNeese, Tim. *The Oregon Trail: Pathway to the West*. New York: Chelsea House Publishers, 2009.

The Oregon Trail
<http://www.america101.us/trail/Oregontrail.html>
> *This website is based on the award-winning documentary film from PBS. Read about the history of the trail and see the historic sites located along the way.*

The Oregon Territory and its Pioneers
<http://www.america101.us/trail/Oregontrail.html>
> *This site offers information on the pioneers of the Oregon Territory up to and including 1855.*

History Globe: Map of Oregon Trail
<http://www.historyglobe.com/ot/otmap1.htm>
> *Use this map of the Oregon Trail to capture images and historic sites.*

INDEX